T0045425

Bottom of the World 2
by Michael Bilski

The Heroic Age of Antarctic Exploration . . . 4
by Michael Bilski

Andrew's Antarctic Adventure 16
by Michael Bilski

Discuss 24

GENRE Haiku

Read to find out about Antarctica.

Bottom of the World

by Michael Bilski

Imagine a world that gets less than one inch of **precipitation** during the year. Think of it, hardly any drizzle, rain, snow, or sleet in one entire year. Picture icy mountains, some more than three miles high. The average **temperature** during the coldest month is between −40°F and −94°F (−40°C and −70°C). Now that is cold! What and where is this place? It's the **continent** of Antarctica, land of the **South Pole.** This is the frozen desert at the bottom of the world.

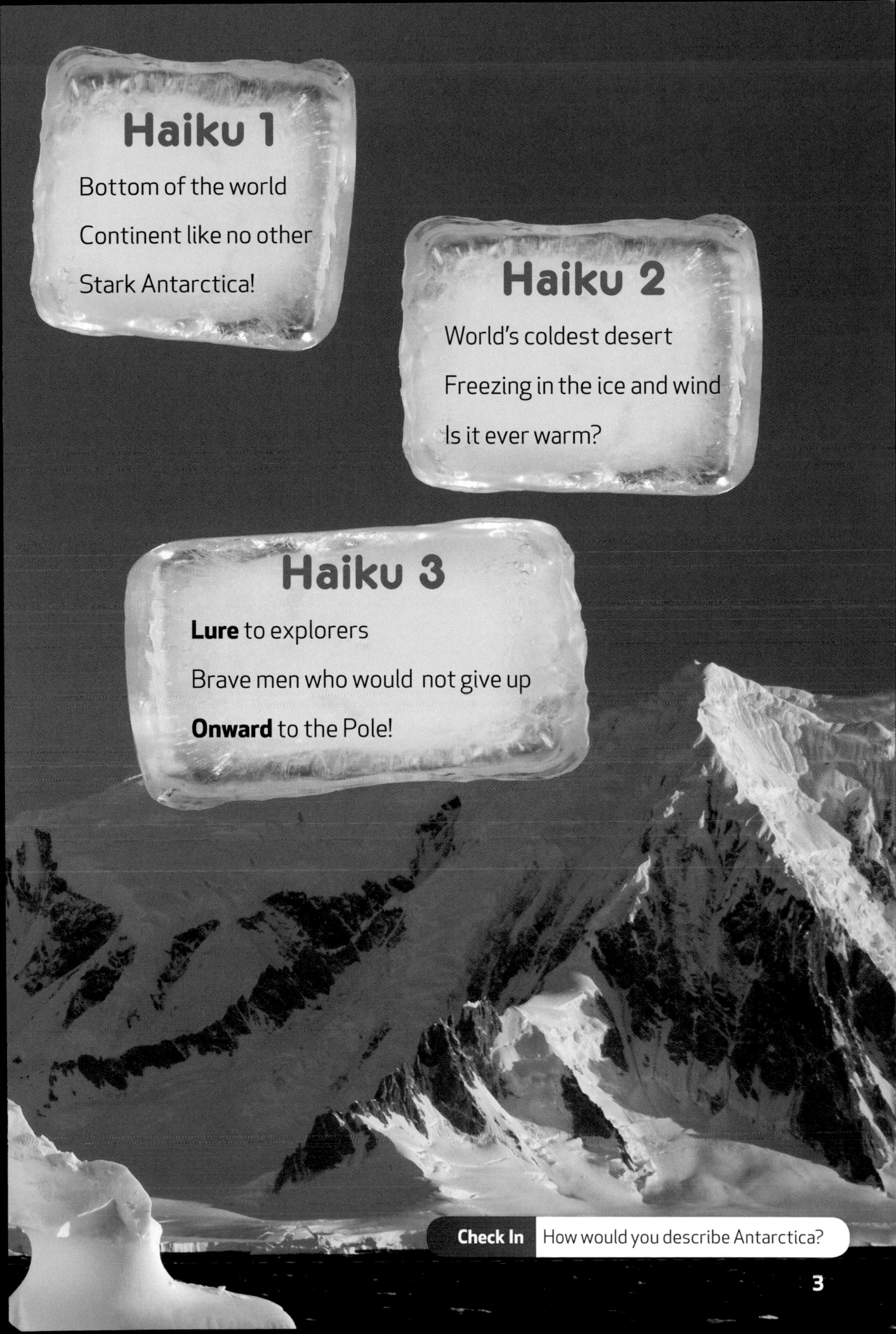

Haiku 1

Bottom of the world
Continent like no other
Stark Antarctica!

Haiku 2

World's coldest desert
Freezing in the ice and wind
Is it ever warm?

Haiku 3

Lure to explorers
Brave men who would not give up
Onward to the Pole!

Check In How would you describe Antarctica?

GENRE History Article

Read to find out about early Antarctic explorers.

The Heroic Age of Antarctic Exploration

by Michael Bilski

There was a time when Antarctica was a whole new world to explore. The time from just before 1900 until 1922 was called the Heroic Age of Antarctic Exploration. During that time, brave men explored the **continent.** These explorers from all over the world faced bitter cold and terrible conditions. Something in these men made them press **onward.** Roald Amundsen, Robert Falcon Scott, and Ernest Shackleton were three such explorers.

Antarctic Explorers

Erich von Drygalski

German South Polar Expedition, 1901–1903

Roald Amundsen

Norwegian Antarctic Expedition, 1910–1912

First to reach South Pole (December 14, 1911)

Adriene de Gerlache

Belgian Antarctic Expedition, 1897–1899

William Speirs Bruce

Scottish National Antarctic Expedition, 1902–1904

Ernest Shackleton

British Antarctic Expedition, 1907–1909

Imperial Trans-Antarctic Expedition, 1914–1917

Shackleton-Rowett Expedition, 1921–1922

Carsten Borchgrevink

British Antarctic Expedition, 1898–1900

Jean-Baptiste Charcot

French Antarctic Expedition, 1903–1905 and 1908–1910

Nobu Shirase

Japanese Antarctic Expedition, 1910–1912

Nils Otto Nordenskjold

Swedish South Polar Expedition, 1901–1903

Robert Falcon Scott

British National Antarctic Expedition, 1901–1904

British Antarctic Expedition, 1910–1913

Reached South Pole (January 17, 1912)

Douglas Mawson

Australasian Antarctic Expedition, 1911–1914

Rival Explorers

Roald Amundsen

Roald Amundsen was born in Norway in 1872. He explored the polar Arctic region and wanted to be the first to reach the **North Pole.** In the cold north, Amundsen learned how the Inuit survived. He began to wear reindeer clothing as they did. He also learned about using sled dogs. When other explorers discovered the North Pole before Amundsen, he decided that he would be the first to reach the **South Pole.** He knew that Robert Scott had the same goal. The race was on!

Robert Falcon Scott

Robert Falcon Scott was born in England in 1868. He was barely a teen when he began his career in the navy. Scott's first **expedition** to Antarctica took place from 1901 to 1904. Scott and his team came within 400 miles of the South Pole. Scott was determined to lead the first expedition to reach the South Pole, and he returned to Antarctica in 1911. He was disappointed to learn that Amundsen had the same goal, but Scott would not give up.

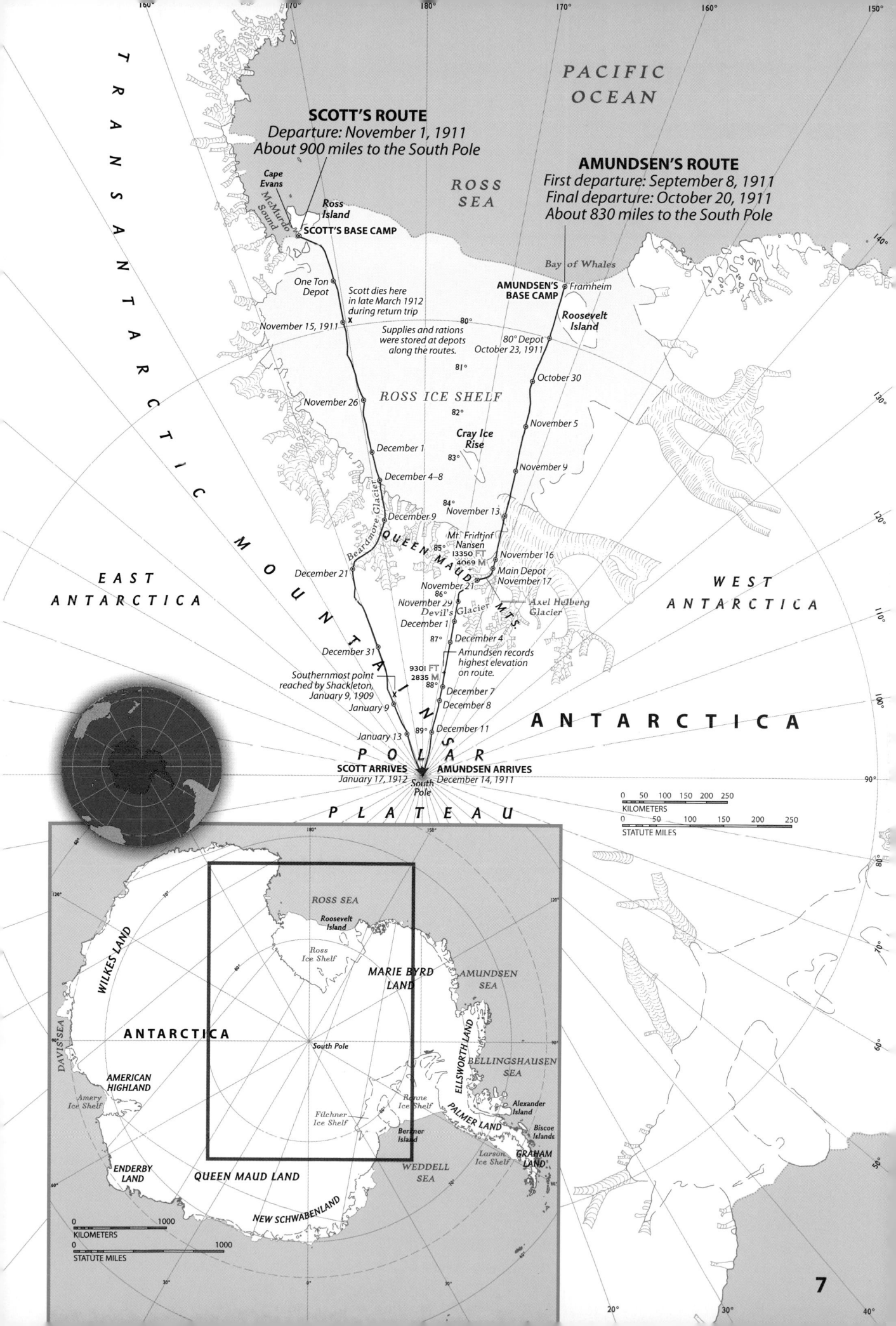
PACIFIC OCEAN
SCOTT'S ROUTE
Departure: November 1, 1911
About 900 miles to the South Pole
AMUNDSEN'S ROUTE
First departure: September 8, 1911
Final departure: October 20, 1911
About 830 miles to the South Pole
ROSS SEA
Cape Evans
McMurdo Sound
Ross Island
SCOTT'S BASE CAMP
Bay of Whales
AMUNDSEN'S BASE CAMP
Framheim
Roosevelt Island
One Ton Depot
Scott dies here in late March 1912 during return trip
November 15, 1911
Supplies and rations were stored at depots along the routes.
80° Depot October 23, 1911
October 30
ROSS ICE SHELF
November 26
November 5
Cray Ice Rise
December 1
November 9
December 4–8
November 13
Beardmore Glacier
December 9
QUEEN MAUD MTS
Mt. Fridtjof Nansen 13350 FT 4069 M
November 16
December 21
Main Depot November 17
November 21
November 29
Devil's Glacier
Axel Heiberg Glacier
December 1
December 4
December 31
Amundsen records highest elevation on route.
9301 FT 2835 M
Southernmost point reached by Shackleton, January 9, 1909
December 7
January 9
December 8
January 13
December 11
TRANSANTARCTIC MOUNTAINS
EAST ANTARCTICA
WEST ANTARCTICA
ANTARCTICA
POLAR PLATEAU
SCOTT ARRIVES January 17, 1912
AMUNDSEN ARRIVES December 14, 1911
South Pole
0 50 100 150 200 250 KILOMETERS
0 50 100 150 200 250 STATUTE MILES
ROSS SEA
Roosevelt Island
Ross Ice Shelf
MARIE BYRD LAND
AMUNDSEN SEA
WILKES LAND
ANTARCTICA
South Pole
DAVIS SEA
ELLSWORTH LAND
BELLINGSHAUSEN SEA
AMERICAN HIGHLAND
Amery Ice Shelf
Ronne Ice Shelf
Alexander Island
PALMER LAND
Filchner Ice Shelf
Berkner Island
Biscoe Islands
Larsen Ice Shelf
GRAHAM LAND
ENDERBY LAND
QUEEN MAUD LAND
WEDDELL SEA
NEW SCHWABENLAND
0 1000 KILOMETERS
0 1000 STATUTE MILES

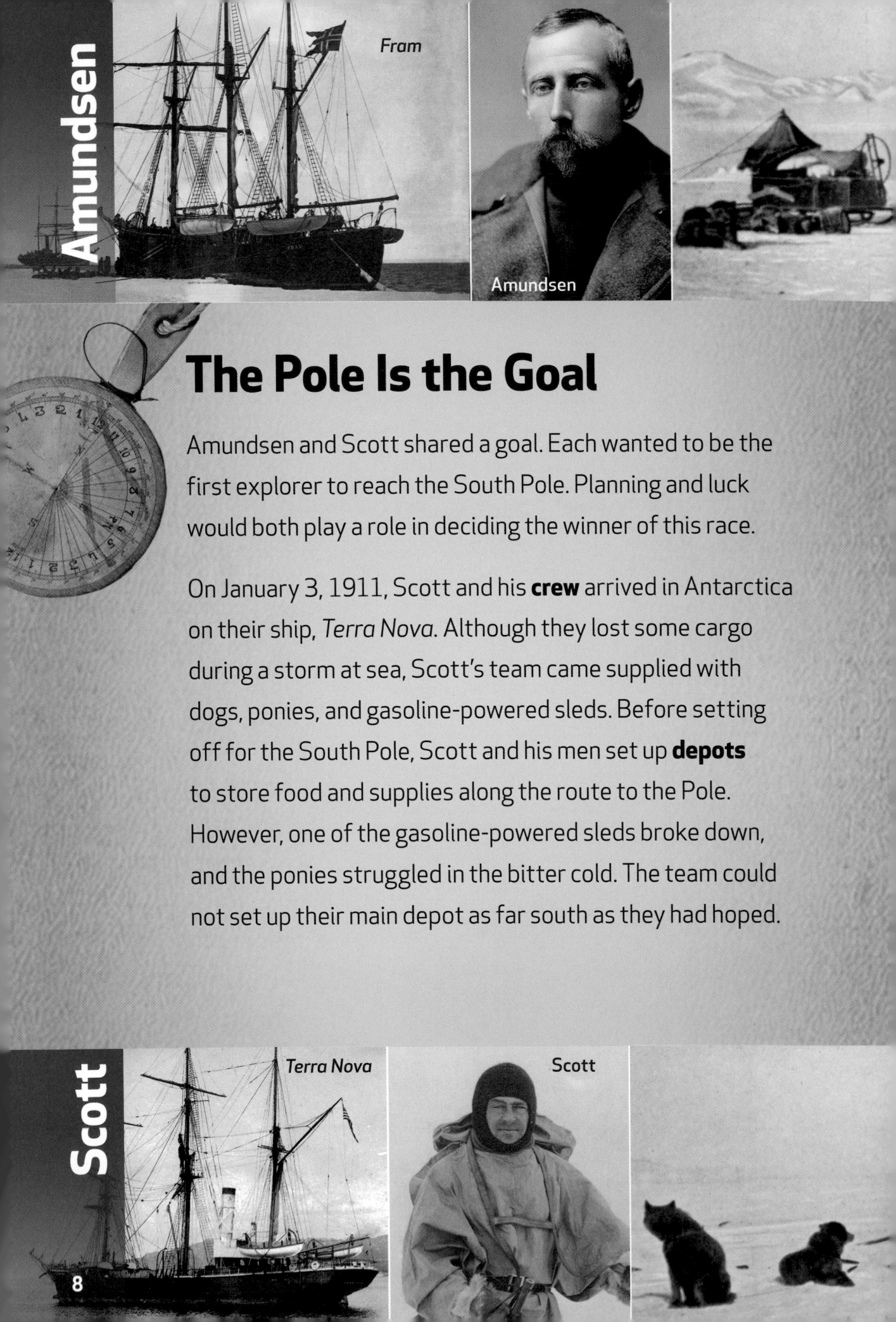

The Pole Is the Goal

Amundsen and Scott shared a goal. Each wanted to be the first explorer to reach the South Pole. Planning and luck would both play a role in deciding the winner of this race.

On January 3, 1911, Scott and his **crew** arrived in Antarctica on their ship, *Terra Nova*. Although they lost some cargo during a storm at sea, Scott's team came supplied with dogs, ponies, and gasoline-powered sleds. Before setting off for the South Pole, Scott and his men set up **depots** to store food and supplies along the route to the Pole. However, one of the gasoline-powered sleds broke down, and the ponies struggled in the bitter cold. The team could not set up their main depot as far south as they had hoped.

Sled at a supply depot

On January 14, 1911, Amundsen and his crew arrived in Antarctica on their ship, *Fram*. They set up base camp on the Ross Ice Shelf. They would stay there for nine months, preparing for the trek to the South Pole.

Amundsen was prepared with supplies and fresh water. He remembered what he had learned from the Inuit. He knew skis and dogs would help him in his quest. He brought almost 100 sled dogs to Antarctica. Amundsen and his crew spent weeks moving supplies and food from *Fram* to the camp. They set up depots with food along the trail to the Pole. As the men waited for the weather to improve in spring, they practiced and prepared. They trained the dogs. They practiced skiing. The men used the trained dogs and sleds to get their supply depots closer to the Pole than Scott could. Amundsen also made sure his men and dogs were well-fed and rested for the trip ahead.

Dog team

Testing the sea's depth with a hammer

Amundsen's team at the South Pole

Victory and Defeat

On October 20, 1911, Amundsen set off for the South Pole. His crew included a champion skier and two expert dog drivers. They took four sleds and more than 50 dogs. The food depots did the trick. The men skied and the dogs pulled the sleds. The team used stones to mark the trail. Climbing mountains and battling blizzards, the frostbitten men and dogs pressed onward. Finally, on December 14, 1911, they reached the Pole! There was no sign of Scott. The race was won. Amundsen and his men celebrated their victory. They planted a flag and set up a tent. Inside the tent, Amundsen left a note for Scott.

Scott left base camp on November 1, 1911. With him and his crew were 10 ponies, sleds, and more than 20 dogs. The gasoline-powered sleds failed. The ponies struggled in the ice and snow. The team faced bitter cold and endless snow. A blizzard held them up for four days. Scott's team had to

Both explorers chose their teams and equipment differently.

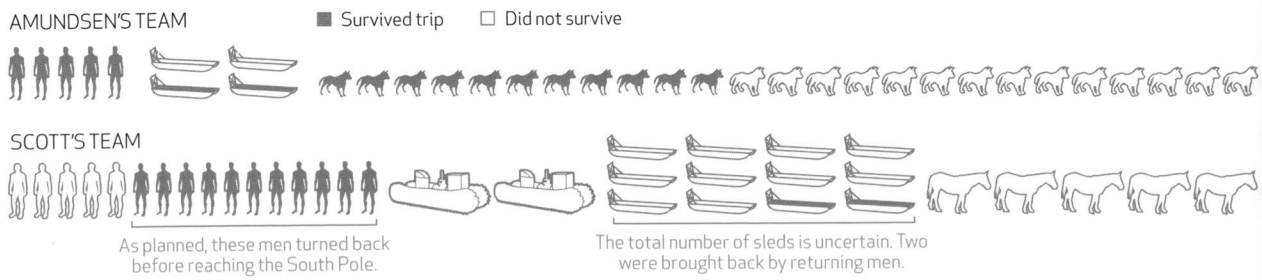

Crossing a glacier on foot

Scott's team at the Pole, with Amundsen's tent and flag

march on foot. They were not capable skiers, and they had to pull their own sleds. As they traveled toward the South Pole, Scott sent the dogs and most of the men back to base camp. He decided to take four men the rest of the way. On January 16, 1912, they saw something that made their hearts sink. In the distance, Amundsen's tent and flag came into view. They knew they had lost the race. When they reached the South Pole on January 17, they found what Amundsen had left for them, including some much-needed supplies.

Amundsen and his team had made it back safely, but Scott's team was less fortunate. They were starving, ill, and exhausted. The remaining men were trapped by a blizzard, 11 miles from their largest depot. They never made it there. Scott's final diary entry finished the sad story.

"We shall stick it out to the end, but we are getting weaker, of course, and the end cannot be far. It seems a pity, but I do not think I can write more."

All surviving dogs were brought back by returning team members.

Shackleton's Endurance

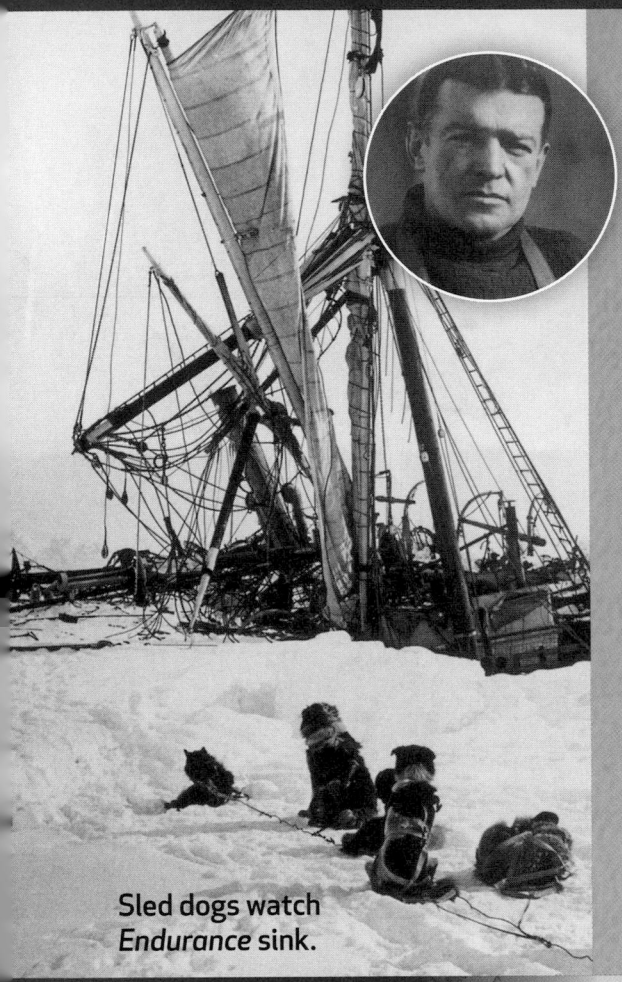

Sled dogs watch *Endurance* sink.

Ernest Henry Shackleton

Ernest Henry Shackleton was born in 1874 in Ireland. He was a member of Scott's crew during Scott's first attempt to reach the South Pole in 1901. In 1908, Shackleton led his own expedition and set a record by getting closer to the South Pole than anyone had before that time.

After Amundsen won the race to the South Pole, Shackleton decided to try something new. He would cross Antarctica on foot. The plan was to start from the Weddell Sea

This map traces their route.

60° 50° 40° 30°

South Georgia Island

Endurance *departs for Antarctica Dec. 5, 1914*

Crew of six lands May 10, 1916

Crew of six departs in search of rescue April 24, 1916

Elephant Island

Lifeboats reach island April 15, 1916

Lifeboats launched from loose pack ice April 9, 1916

0 100 200 300 400 500 KILOMETERS

0 100 200 300 400 500 MILES

SOLID PACK ICE

ATLANTIC OCEAN

ANTARCTIC CIRCLE

ANTARCTIC PENINSULA

Endurance *sinks Nov. 21, 1915*

Endurance *crushed by pack ice Oct. 27, 1915*

LOOSE PACK ICE

Endurance *enters loose pack ice Dec. 11, 1914*

BELLINGSHAUSEN SEA

110°

WEDDELL SEA

Endurance *trapped in solid pack ice Jan. 19, 1915*

120°

RONNE ICE SHELF

80°

WEST ANTARCTICA

ANTARCTICA

130°

20°

10

0

10

and cross a completely unexplored region of Antarctica. The expedition would head to the Pole and then to the Ross Sea.

Shackleton and his men spotted Antarctica. Before Shackleton reached Antarctica, his ship, *Endurance*, became trapped in a drifting pack ice. It was a fatal blow to the expedition. For ten long months, the pack ice held the ship in its powerful clutches. Meanwhile Shackleton and his men used *Endurance* as their base and storage facility. But the ice was slowly crushing the doomed ship, and supplies and lifeboats eventually had to be removed. On November 21, 1915, *Endurance* was crushed and later sank.

Still trapped on the dangerous pack ice, Shackleton and his crew drifted for another five months. The men and dogs endured bitter cold. They survived partly on whale and seal meat. Finally, in their small lifeboats, Shackleton's men were able to escape the ice and get safely to Elephant Island.

Shackleton and his men were trapped on the ice. They didn't set foot on land for more than a year.

Shackleton decided the only hope for rescue was to get one of the lifeboats to the open sea and sail to the nearest inhabited island. It was a dangerous mission. With a crew of five men, Shackleton sailed 800 miles to South Georgia Island. There, they found a ship that could bring them back to rescue the remaining crew. After several unsuccessful attempts, every member of Shackleton's expedition was finally rescued on August 30, 1916. The men had been away from home for more than two years.

The expedition was a failure, but the story of *Endurance* had a heroic end. True to the name of their ship, Shackleton and his fellow explorers had endured.

In 1921 Shackleton reunited with some members of the *Endurance* crew. The plan was to sail a new ship, *Quest*, all the way around Antarctica. Shackleton suffered a heart attack while on board *Quest*. He was buried on South Georgia Island.

Shackleton's crew on board *Quest*

End of the Heroic Age

Shackleton's death marked the end of this heroic age. The final continent had been explored, and both Amundsen and Scott had reached the South Pole. Exploration of a different kind continues to this day. Scientists from all over the world have set up research stations to study this frozen land.

Endurance

Check In What did Scott, Amundsen, and Shackleton have in common? How were they different?

GENRE Third-Person Narrative **Read to find out** about Andrew's journey to Antarctica.

Meet Andrew Evans, National Geographic's "Digital Nomad." A nomad is a traveler, which is what Andrew is. He's a digital nomad because he uses technology to communicate about his travels.

Andrew Evans

Andrew wanted to explore **Antarctica,** much like the explorers of the Heroic Age of Antarctic Exploration. Instead of sailing to Antarctica, Andrew traveled most of the way by bus. People followed Andrew's journey on his **blog.** He kept busy posting news for them every day.

Andrew's Antarctic Adventure

by Michael Bilski

In the first decades of the 20th century, the explorers Amundsen, Scott, and Shackleton used navigation instruments, such as a compass and sextant, to find their way toward the **South Pole**. They recorded their journeys using large box cameras.

Andrew and other explorers today have tools that use GPS, which stands for "Global Positioning System." GPS receivers, digital cameras, and the Internet help explorers find their way and keep a record of their journey. Andrew travels light, but he always takes several small cameras with him, including a favorite waterproof one.

Tools

Present	Past
 *Cell-phone compass*	 *Compass*
 *GPS receiver*	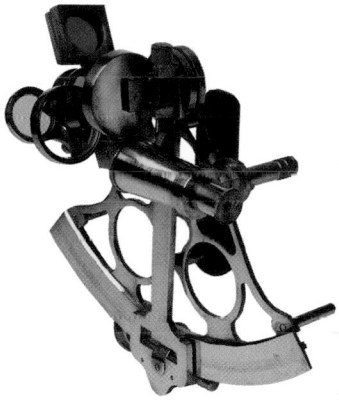 *Sextant*
 *Waterproof camera*	 *Box camera*

Heading South

On January 1, 2010, Andrew got on the bus outside the National Geographic offices in Washington, D.C. Before beginning his long journey, Andrew had asked blog readers to help him pick songs for the ultimate playlist. The songs helped pass the time on the long ride.

UNITED STATES

MEXICO

BELIZE

GUATEMALA

HONDURAS

EL SALVADOR

NICARAGUA

COSTA RICA

PANAMA

ATLANTIC OCEAN

VENEZUELA

COLOMBIA

ECUADOR

PERU

BRAZ

The sunny beaches Andrew hoped to see along the Mexican coastline were gray and colorless because of rain. But he did see white egrets and purple-black grackles.

In Costa Rica, Andrew saw mountain streams, macaws, toucans, and crocodiles, all from his bus window.

The first place Andrew visited in South America was Cartagena, Colombia. Cartagena is a walled city with narrow, cobbled streets and old Spanish buildings. Every house, door, and shutter is a different color.

Ecuador is where Andrew crossed the **Equator**. He walked along the line between North and South, with one foot in each hemisphere.

PACIFIC OCEAN

BOLIVIA

PARAG

The road in and out of La Paz, Bolivia, was over 13,500 feet in elevation. That's more than two miles high! In Southern Bolivia, Andrew saw the spectacular Uyuni salt flats. These flats make up the world's largest salt desert.

When Andrew crossed the border from Ecuador to Peru, the land changed from a tropical jungle to a desert. Here the Sechura Desert meets the Pacific Ocean to the west and the Andes Mountains to the east.

CHILE

URUGUAY

ARGENTINA

The final bus ride through Argentina was more than 3100 miles. Andrew traveled through Cordoba, then **onward** to Ushuaia in Tierra del Fuego. Rough seas in the Strait of Magellan made the short ferry ride pretty scary.

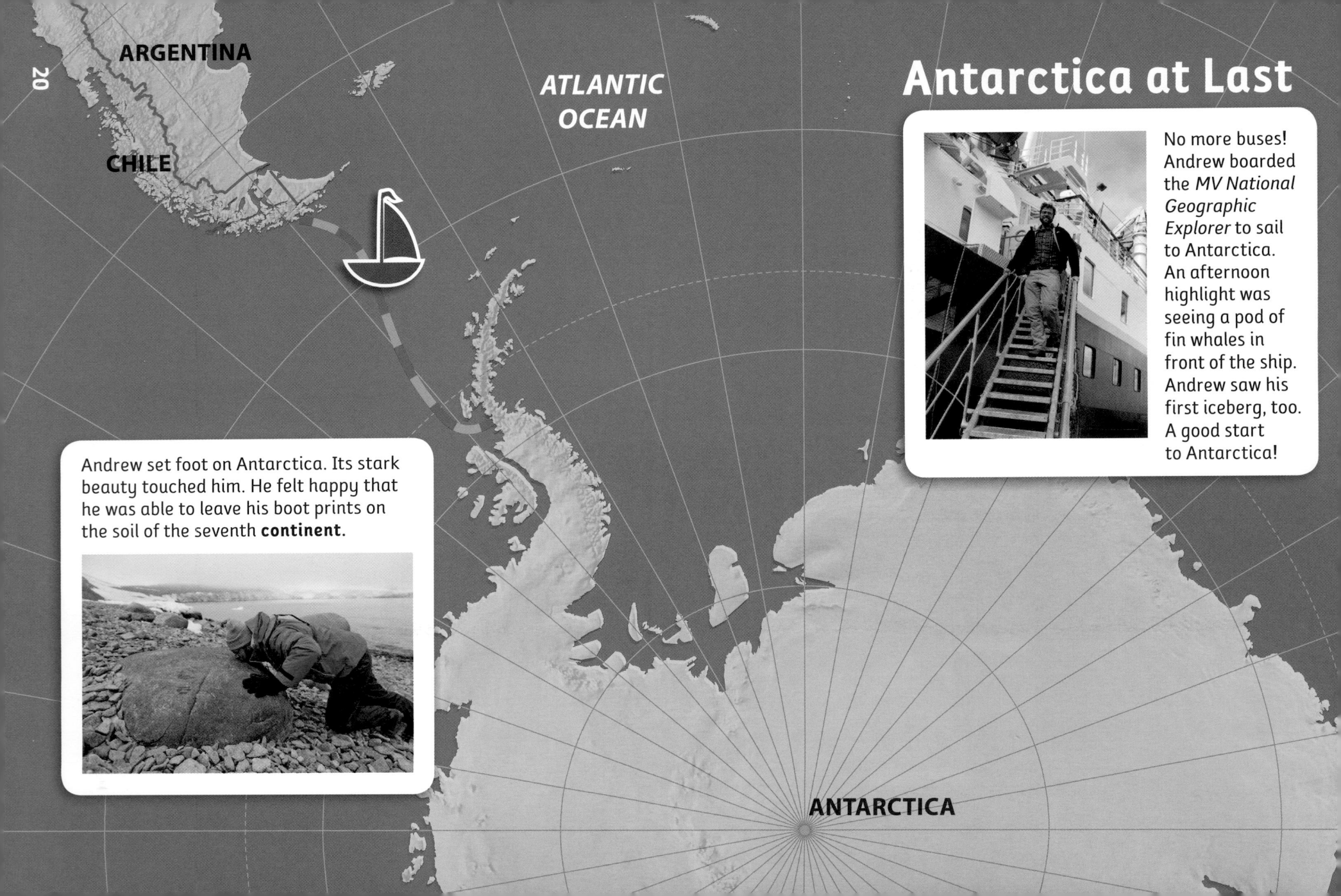

Antarctica at Last

No more buses! Andrew boarded the *MV National Geographic Explorer* to sail to Antarctica. An afternoon highlight was seeing a pod of fin whales in front of the ship. Andrew saw his first iceberg, too. A good start to Antarctica!

Andrew set foot on Antarctica. Its stark beauty touched him. He felt happy that he was able to leave his boot prints on the soil of the seventh **continent**.

PACIFIC OCEAN

The rules for visitors to Antarctica say that you cannot touch any wildlife. You need to stay 15 feet away from the animals at all times. On a visit to the Gentoo penguin colony at Port Lockroy, a baby penguin jumped into Andrew's lap. Then another one came. It was all he could do to obey the rules and not cuddle the penguins.

On the island of South Georgia, Andrew snapped this picture of a very rare all-black penguin. Its rare coloring is called melanism. Melanism happens when increased melanin in the body causes dark pigmentation on the skin, fur, or feathers.

Andrew visited Deception Island, a volcanic crown hollowed out from the inside. The whole island is the mouth of a volcano. On the beach at Deception Island, Andrew did something unusual. He went for a swim. Since the water was 36°F (2°C), he didn't stay in long.

Andrew traveled through 14 countries and covered 10,000 miles in 10 weeks! His trip began on a bus in Washington, D.C. It ended on the continent of Antarctica.

Andrew, like the explorers of the Heroic Age of Antarctic Exploration, set his sights on a destination. He dealt with bumps along the way, but he always managed to press onward. It's what explorers do.

Check In What did you find most interesting about Andrew's trip?

Discuss Compare and Contrast

1. What do you think connects the three pieces that you read in this book? What makes you think that?

2. Compare and contrast the reasons why Amundsen, Scott, Shackleton, and Evans went to Antarctica. How were their reasons alike and different?

3. Andrew Evans uses modern tools, such as a GPS device and a cell phone. How might modern tools have changed the other explorers' expeditions?

4. Choose a haiku. Then find a passage or a photo in another piece that explains or shows what the haiku is describing. Tell how they are connected.

5. What questions do you still wonder about Antarctica or its explorers?